He Waited

He Waited

*The best God has for you,
IS worth waiting for.*

by LaDonna Cooper

HE WAITED

©2014 by LaDonna Cooper
All Rights Reserved.

Published by:

Healthy Life Press • 9375 Blue Mountain Dr. • Golden, CO 80403
www.healthylifepress.com

Cover and Internal Designs: Judy Johnson
Printed in the United States of America

No part of this publication may be reproduced, stored in a retrieval system, or transmitted in any form or by any means—for example, electronic, photocopy, recording—without the prior written permission of the author, except for brief quotations in printed reviews.

Library of Congress Cataloging-in-Publication Data
Cooper, LaDonna
He Waited
ISBN 978-1-939267-79-5
1. Christian Life – Personal Growth

Undesignated Scripture references are taken from THE HOLY BIBLE, NEW INTERNATIONAL VERSION®, NIV® Copyright © 1973, 1978, 1984, 2011 by Biblica, Inc.® Used by permission. All rights reserved worldwide. Texts marked KJV are from the King James Version of the Bible. Certain texts appear in bold type for emphasis.

Most Healthy Life Press resources are available in printed or electronic forms worldwide through bookstores and online outlets, depending on their format. This book is for sale in printed form and in a downloadable and printable eBook PDF format from *www.healthylifepress.com*. Printed books and eBook for "Kindle" are available at: *Amazon.com*, and at: *www.DeeperShopping.com* in printed and various eBook formats. "Nook" reader eBooks are available at *BN.com*. Redistribution of printed or eBook formatted copies, regardless of their source, without written authorization from the copyright holder violates international copyright law, and is strictly forbidden.

Contact: *info@healthylifepress.com* for information about permissions and discounts for booksellers or multiple copy purchases.

This book is dedicated in loving memory of my Uncle Kenneth "Woody" Cooper

Acknowledgments

I thank God for the favor and gifts he has bestowed upon my life. His presence is awesome and *his* promises never lie. It is because of God that I am immensely blessed and abundantly honored to be in the kingdom.

God has blessed me with amazing parents who always support, love, and nurture me. Shannon and Donald Cooper are the glue that God uses to hold our family together. My Dad, who taught me how to recognize my man of God when he comes and my Mom, my number one fan, are my greatest inspiration.

My sisters Jacquelyn, Kendra, and LaVon motivate me to become a better me, and a greater example by being a virtuous woman of God.

Eboni Warren, your tenacity and positive attitude for life, challenges me to grow.

Lastly, to all of my family, spiritual sisters, friends, and church family because you have helped mold my life experiences by being a part of my spiritual journey. I appreciate and love each of you.

Contents

He Waited	1
Is That You?	5
Renewed Song	13
Awakened	19
New Chapter	25
Appointed Time	29
Remix	35
Today	43
MVP	47
Promise	55
Trust	61
True Reveal	67
First Love	75
Healthy Life Press Resources	80

My heart leaped today
at the thought of you loving me,

I almost looked behind me, just to see

If you were gazing somewhere,
looking for someone else,
afraid to acknowledge that perhaps
you were really longing for me

To be more in your presence
under your care

Letting me know that favor ain't fair.

1
He Waited

*Do not be anxious about anything,
but in everything, by prayer and petition,
with thanksgiving, present your requests
to God. And the peace of God, which
transcends all understanding, will guard
your hearts and your minds in Christ Jesus.
Philippians 4:6-7*

Why is it often so challenging for us to wait. We don't like to wait in line at the grocery store, wait in traffic, and we certainly do not like waiting on people who fail to get with our agenda. It is little wonder that we enter relationships, purchase homes, and quit or begin jobs with little reflection or guidance from God. Simply because we often fail to wait to hear his voice; I know because I have been guilty of this as well.

Even when we were little, many of us would want to cross the street alone, only to hear a parent or guardian say, "Wait! Let me hold your hand!" If we had not listened an automobile could have hit us and there could have been major consequences. Often in our naivety even in our adult lives God is saying the same thing, "Let me hold your hand. Wait! There is trouble ahead. If you will just wait, I have something better for you!" But often we forge ahead and do what we want, anyway.

And I for one am very much a go-getter. When I see something I want and I know I am deserving of it, I make the necessary plans to go get it. So often, when things don't go according to my plans, I finally give up and go to God, the ONLY one with a plan that I trust to follow. **Wait** for **the LORD**; be strong and take heart and **wait** for **the LORD** (Psalm 21:14).

You glanced my way today
and held my heart with your stare

But I was so busy I hardly noticed

All I knew was that it was hard to focus

And when you smiled at me
with your eyes I knew that you
were my answered prayer.

Is That You?

*Take delight in the LORD, and he will
give you the desires of your heart.*
Psalm 37:4

I must admit that although I have never looked for a man, I have had plenty of intimate conversations with the Lord concerning what I wanted and needed in a man. I didn't just want a good man, I wanted a GOOD-GOD man, and every day I made sure to remind the Lord that my GOOD-GOD man seemed to be missing in action! I mean, many tried to apply for the position but none seemed to be qualified.

Long ago, I came to the conclusion that there are a

few things that I am extremely selective about; my food, my clothes, and my man! And somehow, I felt like God had missed my memo or misread the invoice because my special delivery had yet to be delivered. So daily, I questioned and tried to justify to the LORD why I was ready to be a wife and WHY I couldn't understand how **he** could be keeping my husband from me.

I complained of my dilemma to my sister-friend, expecting her to be on my side. But instead she said, "What makes you think God is going to send you somebody right now? You are going to mess that man up, and God loves you and your future husband too much to allow your wishes to override God's infinite knowledge."

Needless to say, that is not what I was expecting and I was a bit indignant, letting her know that I was well accomplished with my own home, my own business, and finishing up my PhD. What was she talking about? I was fabulous in my own eyes; was she blind? Even the Bible backed me. "Praise **you** because I am **fearfully and wonderfully made**; your works are wonderful, I know that full well" (see Psalm 139:14). How was I a mess?

Now I wasn't getting it twisted, I knew that the reason why I had accomplished so much was only because God had blessed me with a favored life. I also knew that great responsibility came with such a blessing. "But the one who does not know and does things deserving punishment will be beaten with few blows.

From everyone who has been given much, much will be demanded; and from the one who has been entrusted with much, much more will be asked" (see Luke 12:48).

I understood the structure of the kingdom, so I couldn't understand what the hold up was or more importantly why my husband was being held up! I made up in mind that in my list of accomplishments that a husband was the next thing on my checklist. You may have a similar list:

> Education ✓
> Car ✓
> House ✓
> Start up Business ✓
> Realizing my purpose ✓

But there was one thing missing at this juncture in my life and that was my *husband*.

However, in order to bring me back to reality my friend reminded me that I was focusing more on a preconstructed timeline of my husband finding me than I was focusing on the true prize, which was seeking my first true love. "But **seek first** his **kingdom** and his righteousness, and all these things will be given to you as well" (Matthew 6:33).

I had missed the point and had begun a checklist of man-made things and not the spiritual checklist that was God-inspired. But according to Galatians

5:22-23, the fruit of Spirit is:
- Love ✓
- Joy ✓
- Peace ✓
- Patience ✓
- Kindness ✓
- Goodness ✓
- Faithfulness ✓
- Gentleness ✓
- Self-Control ✓

I was instantly convicted, STILL MAD, but I was convicted and convinced that my friend was right. I came to the full realization that in all of my daily complaint sessions with God, I had lost focus and forgotten to give GOD my undivided attention. How could I dare promise to love and provide all of my attention to a husband when I had not first made God my husbandman? "For **your** Maker is **your husband**—the Lord Almighty is his name—the Holy One of Israel is your Redeemer; he is called the God of all the earth" (Isaiah 54:5).

I had neglected God and for that I was immensely sorry and immediately repented. I realized that it wasn't really about getting my husband, but about control. And as long as I wanted to control my life, then I wasn't following God's blueprint for my life, but was being controlled by my own personal notions and plans. Since then, I have learned to wait on God. "Trust in the Lord with all **your** heart and **lean not** on **your own understanding**; in all **your** ways submit to him, and he will make your paths straight" (Proverbs 3:5-6).

Thank God HE WAITED!

Spiritual Reflections

In what ways, if any, have you made the things in your life a priority over a relationship with God? Read Galatians 5:7-9: "Ye **did** run well; who **did hinder** you that ye should not obey the truth? This persuasion cometh not of him that calleth you. A little leaven leaveneth the whole lump" (KJV). **How does this Scripture apply to your life?**

_____

_____

_____

_____

_____

_____

_____

_____

_____

_____

It wasn't until today that I realized
my song had returned

Ricocheted from the deep crevices
of my heart where it had been lodged
in hurt and pain, returning with
a melody that was stronger, wiser,
and bolder from lessons learned

Not sure when it happened or how

But I can hear the melody
more clearly now.

Renewed Song

*The Lord is my strength and my shield;
my heart trusts in him, and I am helped.
My heart leaps for joy and I will
give thanks to him in song.*
Psalm 28:7

When I was little, I always took comfort in singing, "Yes, Jesus loves me!" I would sing my little heart out as loud as I could because I knew beyond a shadow of a doubt that the Lord heard me and was nodding his head in enjoyment. In fact, I loved going to church as a child because I loved hearing the choir sing. My sister and I would go home and become our own choir.

And over the summer my cousins and I would play church, imitate the church choir, and pretend to shout. My older cousin even played the part of the preacher. Oh the fun we had! There was nothing we couldn't do. We really took joy in making a joyful noise unto the Lord. "Make a joyful noise unto the Lord, all ye lands. Serve the Lord with gladness: come before his presence with singing. Know ye that the Lord he is God: it is he that hath made us, and not we ourselves; we are his people, and the sheep of his pasture" (Psalm 100:1-3).

With that being said, I'm not sure when the melody changed or when I lost my heart to enjoy God's symphony. It happened so subtly that I didn't even realize that I had misplaced my song.

I became so busy with what was going on in my life that I forgot to acknowledge the ONE who had given me life. And although I have always known God, somewhere along the way, I had lost focus and God had become a convenient necessity and not my number one priority. As my relationships with people seemed to flourish, my relationship with God seemed to be on standby. I knew HE was always there, but I couldn't say that I was always reciprocating the loyalty.

During that period in my life, I was more focused on doing the right thing because I felt like it was what I was supposed to do and not because it was what I was purposed to do. My life, though seemingly structured, lacked direction because I wasn't always listening to God. "The **LORD** is my strength and my shield; my heart **trusts** in him, and he helps me. My heart leaps for joy, and with my song I praise him" (Psalm 28:7). I had to learn that in all aspects of my life I needed direction and structure.

What happens when one or both are missing? We are often in a constant state of chaos and disorganization. God is a God of order. "But everything should be done in a fitting and orderly way" (1 Corinthians 14:40).

Sometimes, we can become so busy with the things of the world that we become lazy with the things of God. We get caught up in doing the right thing for the wrong motive. When we fail to prioritize our lives with kingdom building and living we run the risk of placing our confidence and hope in man and in the things of this world. "**And be not conformed to this world**: but be ye transformed by the renewing of your mind, that ye may prove what is that good, and acceptable, and perfect, will of God" (Romans 12:2, KJV).

By allowing God to guide our lives we are able to continue life's journey equipped with the greatest road map available and that is through God's personal GPS, the holy living Word of God.

Spiritual Reflections

Have you ever done the right thing for the wrong reason? What was the end result? How can you do things differently in the future?

Today when I closed my eyes,
I saw you; holy, loving, and bold

I blinked but your image did not
disappear for it was imprinted
in my heart and etched in my soul

Your presence ushering to me,
a song I long thought lost
I thought I'd carelessly thrown the
lyrics away, not recognizing the cost

To be more in your presence
under your care

Letting me know that favor ain't fair.

Awakened

Do not arouse or awaken love
until it so desires.
Song of Songs 2:7

Have you ever had that restless feeling that your life is missing something? You innately know that there has to be more to life then what is going on right now. When days begin looking alike and one day merges into the other with no apparent respite or change in sight? The good news is that God hears us. "I **call** on you, my **God**, for you will answer me; turn your ear to me and **hear** my prayer" (Psalm 17:6).

This is when God is speaking to us the loudest.

However, we may not hear as clearly from God if we allow distractions from all the mumbo jumbo going on in our lives, but he is clearly speaking if we allow the clutter from our lives and minds to dissipate. "**Come to me, all** you who are **weary** and burdened, and I will give you rest" (Matthew 11:28).

Sometimes, when are not operating in our calling, we have a restless feeling. It is often the thing that we feel the most passionate about or the thing that irks us the most that will give us the greatest enjoyment, thus creating the greatest fulfillment.

Have you ever awakened, only to want to go back to sleep? Simply going through the motions and not really living life. There are times when we are merely sleepwalking through life, appearing alert but inside only partially awake. Sometimes, the pressures of life can drain the very being of life and the desire to live the life that God intends. It is not until we listen to the voice of God that we realize that he has not forgotten us and that HIS plan is bigger and better than anything that we could imagine. "**Hear** me when I **call**, O **God** of my righteousness: thou hast enlarged me when I was in distress; have mercy upon me, and **hear** my prayer" (Psalm 4:1, KJV).

Spiritual Reflections

What has God been speaking to you about? Perhaps it is a new business venture, a return to school, or a zeal for ministry? Write down your vision and what God says about it. Study the Scriptures to find God's purpose for your life.

I never thought that I'd
revisit this particular book
Didn't plan on giving it a second look

In fact I almost gave up
reading it altogether
But I couldn't stay away, because
reading it always made me feel better

I stared at it for a while
its cover still closed
Waiting for me to open it I suppose

But I ignored the call
and didn't want to read the **Word**
And when the words continued to
beckon, I pretended it wasn't
my name I heard

Instead I sought other advice
when the answers to my questions
were in plain sight
Rejecting God's voice,
refusing to see the light

It wasn't until **he** spoke
that "My Grace is sufficient."
That my will bent,
and I began to repent.

Accepting that a new chapter had begun
Leaving the past hurt behind,
because the former chapter
had been re-written
and that song would never be re-sung.

New Chapter

*Finally, be strong in the Lord
and in his mighty power. Put on the
full armor of God so that you can
take your stand against the devil's schemes.*
Ephesians 6:10-11

It is an amazing gift to know that despite our past mistakes that God still loves us and wants us to draw closer to him. We will feel extreme disappointment if we allow what the devil says to override God's promises. Therefore we cannot allow the devil's words to embrace us in a death grip, when the loving arms of the Father are open wide to receive us at anytime. It is in the dark places of our lives that God shines forth in his captivating light.

I had to learn that getting honest with God was a lot easier than being honest with people because people often hold grudges and make fast judgment calls. However, God, who knows everything, allows for repentance through his grace and mercy. Yet, even knowing this, there is often a nagging suspicious pull that allows us at times to put on the same façade with God as we do with others, as if God doesn't see through the act. For it is when we are truly open with ourselves and with God that God can pull back the curtain and finish the work that he has begun.

We cannot become so engrossed in perfecting our script that we neglect Scripture. However, we can find comfort in God. Letting us know that whatever bad choices we have made are often bad scenes, HE, the author, can rewrite the script of our lives. "Therefore, if anyone is in Christ, the **new creation** has come: The old has gone, the **new** is here" (2 Corinthians 5:17).

Knowing that God cares for us allows us to fully embrace his love and the predestined role that he has orchestrated just for us.

Spiritual Reflections

Do you feel as if you have disappointed God? What does Scripture say about this? Remember there is a difference between condemnation and conviction. How do we embrace God's love and become free from past mistakes? What Scriptures support God's love?

_____

_____

_____

_____

_____

_____

_____

_____

_____

_____

_____

I thought that you'd forgotten about me,
as you seemed to take so long
I am realizing that I was wrong

I was wrong to assume that because
you didn't give me what I wanted
when I wanted, that you didn't love me

But you weren't rejecting me
 instead you were propelling me
into my destiny.

Appointed Time

*Cast your cares on the Lord
and he will sustain you;
he will never let the righteous fall.
Psalm 55:22*

I've never been a particularly patient person. I figure that if I put the work in then I should be able to dictate what I want and how I want it. And although that philosophy may work with man, it does not work with God because God is sovereign and he knows best. Yet time and time again, I would find myself questioning God's timing. "Be patient, then, brothers and sisters, until the Lord's coming. See how the farmer waits for the land to yield its valuable crop, patiently waiting for the autumn and spring rains. You too, be patient and stand firm, because the Lord's coming is near" (James 5:7-8).

On my checklist of things to do and goals to be completed, I'd find myself agitated with what I felt was God's slow movement. I would look for a sign or some type of confirmation, anything that would convince me that God had at least heard my request. And then I would get mad when it wasn't an answer I wanted to hear.

I'd find myself bargaining with God. I'd start off with something like this, "God, I heard what you said, and I did the work, and I believe I'm ready now." When what I meant was, "I did what you said, Lord, but I'm not happy about it." "Now can I have it?" As if God didn't already know my motives.

Truth be told, I really wasn't as ready as I thought I was. I was doing the right thing with the wrong motives, and then looking at God like he was obligated to bless me when I ended up in a mess.

I am sure God was shaking his head saying, "Why does this child keep asking me the same question in a different way every time? My answer is still the same."

It reminded of when I was little and I would call my Mom for what I thought was a life and death situation, and really I just wanted to hear myself talk. And I figured since she was right there, then she should be happy to stop whatever it was that she was doing and cater to my incessant questions.

At first she was a willing participant but after a while she would be like, "If you'd just wait a minute. Go find something to do while you wait for me." Then I would come back two minutes later ready for my answer and she would say, "Girl, if you don't get somewhere and sit down!"

I know that is probably what the Lord was saying in many instances in my life. However, I learned, and I am still learning, that perhaps I should shift my focus and ask a different question. After all, God doesn't have to report to me. I don't tell him HE tells me! He isn't working on my time, because my time belongs to him, and the sooner I acknowledge that God is already blessing me, the sooner and better prepared I am to receive the answers to the questions I have been asking. This is his way of letting me know that it is not about me and me having to be in control. I am learning that it is not my right to have everything I want when I want it just because I ask for it. That's God's role, so I just have to learn to stay in my lane and adjust my speed on God's roadmap for my life.

Spiritual Reflections

What checklists are you keeping that interfere with God's timeline? (Now we should have goals and standards so that we do not compromise the Word of God, BUT our checklist should never try to dictate God's timing or his love.) What happens when we do things in our timing and refuse to wait on God's timing?

_____

_____

_____

_____

_____

_____

_____

_____

_____

It all seems so familiar but my spirit
senses that something has changed
My thoughts and mindset
have all been rearranged.

I am trusting in God
and following **his** plan
No longer placing my confidence in man
Appreciating my blessings
and loving my Lord
Content to be on one accord

Immersed in his presence
through worship and praise
Forever his lady; no longer caged.

Remix

> *Do not conform any longer to the pattern of this world, but be transformed by the renewing of your mind. Then you will be able to test and approve what God's will is—his good, pleasing, and perfect will.*
> **Romans 12:2**

It is when we give our all to God that we can fully receive and believe ***all*** that he has for us. However, when we are led by our emotions, sometimes we can allow our mistakes to affect our sense of worth to the Lord. For often we may feel as though what we have done has distanced us from God, when in reality, God loves us and welcomes our love and worship. Yet, when we allow the devil to speak into our ear and we do not guard our eye and ear gates, we play Russian roulette with our hearts and freedom. We often second-guess God's love and his ability to love us. Yet, despite what is that we have done, God is a loving God and the devil is a thief that tries to tarnish that love. My aunt says it best, "The devil thinks he's the chief, when really all he is, is a thief!"

God wants to restore not only the natural things in which we have lost but more importantly HE also is able to restore our mind and soul so that our spirit can increase. If we are open to receive HIS love then we are open to express his love through our actions. For God's love is present and speaks to our hearts if we are willing to listen. "I will repay you for the years the locusts have eaten—the great locust and the young locust, the other locusts and the locust swarm—my great army that I sent among you" (Joel 2:25).

We must close the door on negative thinking so that we can receive all that God has for us, because if we are not careful we can talk ourselves out of our blessings and instead walk in defeat. That is not what God intends, for he wishes that we live life in abundance. "Beloved, **I wish above all things that you** may **prosper** and be in health, even as your soul prospers" (3 John 1:2).

When we take the time to think upon all the good things that God has done and is still doing, we realize that he has not forgotten us and that his love has no substitute. "Finally, brothers and sisters, whatever is true, whatever is noble, whatever is right, whatever is pure, whatever is lovely, whatever is admirable—if anything is excellent or praiseworthy—think about such things" (Philippians 4:8).

As such, it is important that we record or acknowledge faith events. "Then the LORD replied: '**Write** down the revelation and **make it plain** on tablets so that a herald may run with it' " (Habakkuk 2:2). These are events where we know that we faithed something and God made it happen. When we do this, we realize that God has bestowed many blessings on us because he loves us, and there is nothing we can do to earn his blessings. We just have to be in a place both spiritually and naturally to receive them.

For I would much rather have God's presence then his presents!

Spiritual Reflections

What in your past are you allowing to keep you from God's presence? Where in your life are you allowing the devil to steal your joy? (Remember: There is nothing that can separate us from the love of God.)

Today my heart skipped a beat...
Twice with elation
As your eyes bore into mine,
smothering my thoughts
with unspoken declaration

Thoughts of love and
breathtaking prayers
Images that manifest
in your awe-taking stares

I forced myself to blink and look away
Because I was afraid to read
what your eyes seemed to say

My heart pounding, I pretended
not to notice, but your gaze refused
to let go, forcing me to acknowledge
your presence, pleading for me
not to go, so I stayed,

Praying that you would
come through on all the promises
your eyes had conveyed.

Too far gone to consider
turning back now
Because in your heart
I've been found.

Today

*Delight yourself in the Lord and he will
give you the desires of your heart.*
Psalm 37:4

The moment when you realize that God has eyes for you is a paramount feeling like no other. It is a miraculous gift to know that we are truly made after God's own image. "So **God** created mankind in his own **image**, in the **image** of **God** he created them; male and female he created them" (Genesis 1:27). The contentment we feel that, among millions of people, if we call and need the Lord that he is ever present and never disappoints. That type of love can't be reduplicated in man but can only be found in the loving gaze and comforting presence of God.

When we understand the value of our lives, we can operate in God's plan for our lives. The real threat is that the devil recognizes our value and seeks to devour us before we can ever realize our truest potential. BUT, the devil is a liar and what God intends will prevail. "Being confident of this, that **he** who began a good **work** in you will carry it on to completion until the day of Christ Jesus" (Philippians 1:6).

We are God's treasure and we have value beyond anything we can dream or imagine. God is not like man and we can never offend God with our first impression. "**Before** I **formed** you in the womb I **knew** you, **before** you **were** born I set you apart; I appointed you as a prophet to the nations" (Jeremiah 1:4-5). There is no surprising God. He knows and still loves us.

The devil *is* a defeated foe who wants to dull our lives with monotony, judgment, fear, and condemnation. But God highlights the good through repentance and erases the bad. "You will again have compassion on us; you will tread our sins underfoot and hurl all our iniquities **into** the depths of **the sea**" (Micah 7:19).

Spiritual Reflections

How can we further recognize the importance of our lives to God and the kingdom? What spiritual gifts do you have that are valuable to the kingdom? If you are not using your gifts, what has prevented you from using your God-given gifts?

_____

_____

_____

_____

_____

_____

_____

_____

_____

_____

_____

_____

Motivating, captivating,
awe-inspiring man of Valor
Because you're an anointed man of God
that's got plenty of swagger

Not boastful or arrogant in his ways
A Man of Vision, Prayer, and Praise.

*But the Lord said to Samuel,
"Do not consider his appearance or
his height, for I have rejected him.
The Lord does not look at the things
man looks at. Man looks at the outward
appearance, but the Lord looks at the heart."
1 Samuel 16:7*

I realized through my journey that my main goal was not to become an independent woman. What I wanted was to trust God and become self-sufficient. "She considers a field and buys it; from her earnings she plants a vineyard" (Proverbs 31:16). My desire to become a helpmeet is because I know God has equipped me with the right tools to be a blessed asset to my future husband. Just as he will help edify I will I help elevate him, for two are better than one because they have a good reward for their labor (see Ecclesiastes 4:9). So in hindsight I am not expecting my husband or anyone else to save me, because Jesus has already done that. I am not expecting a knight in shining armor, I am comforted in knowing he knows how to praise and pray. I know without a doubt that when he loves the Lord and knows how to get into God's presence, he will undoubtedly know how to treat me. "Stand firm then, with the belt of truth buckled around your waist, with the **breastplate of righteousness** in place" (Ephesians 6:14).

But I sometimes allow my logical mind to supercede spiritual wisdom, so although I had the right ingredients I was well on my way to a disaster because I was still trying to figure things out according to the plan I had for life and not necessarily God's plan or his way. "For **my thoughts are not your thoughts**, neither are **your** ways my ways," declares the Lord (Isaiah 55:8).

Sometimes when we are unsure of our standing with God, we seek counsel from anyone and everything other than the Word of God. Blogs, social media, chat rooms, and other media outlets are swarmed with questions from the "cares of the world." "And **the cares** of this **world**, and the deceitfulness of riches, and the lusts of other things entering in, choke the word, and it becometh unfruitful" (Acts 17:11, KJV). Yet, God wants us to seek him and to seek "godly counsel."

God promises to be our counselor. "I will instruct you and teach you in the way you should go; I will counsel you and watch over you" (Psalm 32:8). When we are feeling alone, God wants us to seek a more intimate relationship with him and to draw nearer to him.

You may ask, "How do I do that?" When you are worried, WORSHIP! When you are pained, PRAISE! Scripture describes how God will, ". . . provide for those who grieve in Zion—to bestow on them a crown of beauty instead of ashes, the oil of joy instead of mourning, and a garment of praise instead of a spirit of despair. They will be called oaks of righteousness, a planting of the LORD for the display of his splendor" (Isaiah 61:3).

Just as you would do for your husband or wife or in preparation for a big event in your life, PREPARE! Prepare a place where you are comfortable and spend some alone time with God. Sing, dance, praise, light candles, you choose the mood and the spot because God has already chosen YOU! The important thing is to not wimp out in our wait! "**Wait** for **the Lord**; Be strong, and let your heart take courage; Yes, **wait** for **the Lord**" (Psalm 27:14).

Spiritual Reflections

Has there been a time in your life when you have sought ungodly counsel? Why is it important to seek godly counsel?

Spiritual Reflections

Do you have a quiet place where you can spend time with the Lord? If you do not have a "prayer closet," how do you optimize your time with God so that you can hear his voice and be alone in his presence?

_____

_____

_____

_____

_____

_____

_____

_____

_____

_____

_____

_____

You gave me a promise
but I didn't believe
I never gave it one thought,
lest I be deceived

But you honored your word
and you didn't lie
You let me know instead, that you were
God alone and didn't need man's alibi

I had to listen for your voice
and answer your call
Because I needed you more than ever
and there was no point in trying to stall

So you held me real close
and covered me in prayer
Promising that all my burdens
you would bear

I stepped on out faith
and renewed my trust
Fleeing from temptation
and youthful lusts

Only to hear,
"well done my child!"
The promise now granted,
the wait worthwhile.

Promise

*Being confident of this, that he who began
a good work in you will carry it on to
completion until the day of Christ Jesus.*
Philippians 1:6

If I had a dollar for every time that a coworker, supervisor, or friend tried to hook me up with a family member I could buy a small used car. I got so tired of hearing, "You're such a pretty girl, what are you doing single?" It got to the point that I nearly cringed every time someone asked me if I was dating, as if being single was the equivalent of being "SIN"GLE, emphasis on the "SIN." I could not understand why people were still asking me. Really? If I knew I'd tell them. I was focusing on the "SING" part of "SINGLE." It seemed as though others were more upset about me being single than I was.

At first I really enjoyed my single journey. I met many people and I learned a lot about myself. I was preparing myself. I realized I had work to do and that I was on a mission and that I was enjoying it. I was preparing for the bridegroom, both spiritually and naturally.

"At that time the kingdom of heaven will be like ten virgins who took their lamps and went out to meet the bridegroom. Five of them were foolish and five were wise. The foolish ones took their lamps but did not take any oil with them. The wise ones, however, took oil in jars along with their lamps. The bridegroom was a long time in coming, and they all became drowsy and fell asleep. At midnight the cry rang out: 'Here's the bridegroom! Come out to meet him!'" (Matthew 25:1-6).

But after awhile the incessant questions of well-intentioned people began to get on my nerves. So much so, that I became as perplexed as they were and I began to almost resent the interrogations. I wanted to scream on more than one occasion, "Did you not read my first book where I talked about this?" But in truth, it had been awhile since I had read it, myself, and it was becoming evident by my attitude about single life that I was neglecting to read the most important book, the Bible, as often as I should.

I tried to encourage myself, using the apostle Paul as my example: "I am not saying this because I am in need, for I have learned to be content whatever the circumstances. I know what it is to be in need, and I know what it is to have plenty. I have learned the secret of being content in any and every situation, whether well fed or hungry, whether living in plenty or in want. I can do all this through him who gives me strength" (Philippians 4:11-13). I tried to memorize this Scripture and brand it on my heart. But hey, I didn't know Paul, never dated Paul, and after all, *I wasn't Paul* (LOL)! I truly felt as if my season of singleness was over because my personal goals were already well on their way of being accomplished and I felt as if I was already whole in the Lord.

It wasn't the point that I couldn't get a man. Many attractive men approached me regularly but they didn't seem to be the right men. In fact as soon as they started speaking of long-term commitment, I would mentally begin putting them in the friend zone. I knew it wasn't the right timing and I wasn't where I wanted to be or who I wanted to be in life.

Although I am glad I waited, I was waiting for the wrong reasons. I had to learn that the flaw wasn't necessary in these extraordinary men but in me. The timing wasn't right because I wasn't as ready as I thought I was. My same sister-friend, holding me accountable as always, let me know straight up, "Girl, you are going to find something wrong in every man because you need to allow God to fix you." I didn't know what she meant at the time but when I humbled myself and sought God's voice, I realized she was again partially right (LOL!).

A relationship I thought I was over kept reminding me of what could have been and because of that I left the door partially open, not realizing that until I closed that door, I couldn't allow anyone else to walk through. He knew it was over and I knew it was over and although we both accepted it in good grace, we were still playing a game of cat and mouse where I would hide, hoping he would seek. And as long as I knew he would seek, I was willing to hide, figuring that by the time he counted to ten he would find me, and things would be back to normal. I had to realize that we both were stuck on nine and that we would never get to ten because we just weren't meant to reach ten together.

How many of us are willing to hide how we really feel? We are often one way to family and friends, and another way when we are all alone. However, with God we don't have to hide. God loves us and embraces our tears. "You keep track of all my sorrows. You have collected all my **tears** in your **bottle**. You have recorded each one in your book" (Psalm 56:8). We don't have to fear God's rejection because God is forever present and even without his presents we are embraced and comforted by his presence.

Spiritual Reflections

Are you still leaving a door open that should be closed? (This could include relationships, business partnerships, addictions, and a myriad of other challenges). What does the Word of God say about being free from bondage?

_____

_____

_____

_____

_____

_____

_____

_____

_____

_____

_____

Heartbroken so many times
Disappointed when solace
I couldn't find

Too tired to trust
So fatigued I didn't put up a fuss

I was too tired to think
and too weary to move
Too crumbled to be soothed

It wasn't until I let you in my heart
with an open invitation
That I realized that I was
already free through salvation.

Trust

*But I trust you, O LORD; I say,
"You are my God." My times are in
your hands; deliver me from my enemies
and from those who pursue me.*
Psalm 31:14-15

What is worse than sending a text and getting no reply? Sending a text and having the "read confirmation" option checked on your phone. Which means in short, that your cell phone notifies you when the person reads the text message. So we know the person received the text and we are wondering why they haven't replied. We believers sometimes overanalyze why we feel that

God has not answered our request or prayer. We may begin to think, *God must be busy.*

Isn't it amazing how we often seek confirmation from anyone and everyone else before we seek spiritual confirmation from God. By the time we finally make time for God we have already started rationalizing that perhaps God didn't hear us or get the memo. And this thinking can progress to, *God hasn't answered yet, hence he must not care any more.*

But God is not like man, either in his thinking or what he decides to do and how to do it. "'For my **thoughts** are **not** your **thoughts**, neither are your ways my ways,' declares the LORD" (Isaiah 55:8).

He answers as soon as we ask. However, the delivery may be delayed, for God's good reasons. "Then he said, 'Don't be afraid, Daniel. Since the first day you began to pray for understanding and to humble yourself before your God, your request has been heard in heaven. I have come in answer to your prayer'" (Daniel 10:12).

Our best approach is to wait on the Lord and await his response lest we make decisions based on our own incomplete knowledge and not upon God's infinite wisdom. When our lives are chaotic, it is often more difficult to hear the voice of God. "My sheep listen to my voice; I know them, and they follow me. I give them eternal life, and they shall never perish; no one will snatch them out of my hand. My Father, who has given them to me, is greater than all; no one can snatch them out of my Father's hand. I and the Father are one" (John 10:27-31).

Not hearing God's voice properly may lead to doubt, disbelief in God's promises or timing, or fear. We may fear the unknown, or that if we don't do something to make things happen, it will not get done. Such thinking is harmful because it can create the absence of hope and the false illusion of prosperity or success as being equated with God's love and God's blessings.

However, there is nothing that we can do to earn God's blessings or favor. God's wealth cannot be purchased through good works. "For **by grace** are ye saved through faith; and that not of yourselves: it is **the gift of God**: not of works, **lest any man** should **boast**" (Ephesians 2:8-9, KJV).

God is willing to bless us, but most importantly he is waiting for our love and devotion.

Spiritual Reflections

What do you do when you hear a word from the Lord? How do you know the voice of the Lord? What happens when you don't hear an answer or it isn't the answer you wanted to hear? What Scriptures can you refer to?

_____

_____

_____

_____

_____

_____

_____

_____

_____

_____

_____

_____

He is the color of royal
The epitome of loyal

Protector, lover, and friend
On no other can I depend

A critical part of my destiny
Divine and holy;
bringing out the best in me

Revealing that which is
charitable and true
I found real love in **You**.

True Reveal

*The Lord is gracious and compassionate,
slow to anger and rich in love.*
Psalm 145:8

Who are we really? Sometimes we may portray one thing to the world and quite another to family. Do you remember when you were growing up and you were told not to "act out" in public? We were told not to show off, because to do so would give the impression to the world that we didn't have proper home training. Is it possible that through the years our true selves have been hidden from public display and we have essentially been trained to put on an act? Did we learn to show the world what we want them to see?

Now don't get me wrong, I firmly believe that we should, "**Train up a child** in the way he should go: and when he is old, he will not depart from it" (Proverbs 22:6, KJV). I am not talking about disregarding the Scripture, I am talking about becoming something or someone that we are not, because often in the long run this kind of "acting" can turn into seeking approval from people and keeping up appearances. We can become so engrossed in becoming a "dime piece" that we forget or neglect to give God a tenth of what he asks. "'Bring the whole tithe into the storehouse, that there may be food in my house. Test me in this,' says the LORD Almighty, 'and see if I will not throw open the floodgates of heaven and pour out so much blessing that there will not be room enough to store it'" (Malachi 3:10).

We must find the courage to be ourselves. How? By taking a good long look at ourselves and making sure that what we are reflecting aligns with the Word of God. In this way we are able to confront ourselves and unlock the secrets that we have even fooled ourselves into believing. We cannot hide from the Lord. He already knows of our mistakes and he is waiting for us to come to him. He doesn't want us to hide but to come readily into his presence so that we can accept *his* love and not the world's condemnation. "Then the man and his wife heard the sound of the LORD God as he was walking in the garden in the cool of the day, and they hid from the LORD God among the trees of the garden" (Genesis 3:8).

We cannot allow the devil's lies to become our truth. It is when we are honest with ourselves that we can expose the devil's lies for what they are and walk in divine healing and spiritual growth.

Spiritual Reflections

How important is spiritual discernment? What are we hiding from the world that we *think* we are hiding from God?

Spiritual Reflections

How do we know that God loves and forgives us? What Scripture comforts us in knowing this? How can we be free from the opinion of others?

_____

_____

_____

_____

_____

_____

_____

_____

_____

_____

_____

_____

The image of you was all I needed
and I was amazed
Found myself stumbling
as in a daze

I felt your presence everywhere
and welcomed your embrace
Grateful that for your love
I wouldn't have to chase

For you were accessible and available
And your love proved infallible

Always the gentleman
and comforter of my heart
You captured my soul
and my battles you fought

You never abandoned me
or forgot my name
Promised that the day
I accepted your love, that my life
would never be the same

So you are my first love,
of whom I'll never forget
A blessing, a gift;
truly heaven sent.

First Love

*"'For I know the plans I have for you,'
declares the Lord, 'plans to prosper you and
not to harm you, plans to give you hope and
a future. Then you will call upon me and
come and pray to me, and I will listen to you.
You will seek me and find me when you
seek me with all your heart.'"*
Jeremiah 29:11-13

What are we doing as we wait for our true love? Are we living life to the fullest? In these moments of life we should be encouraging, loving, motivating, and courting the love of our life, relishing the moments where we are able to have intimate quiet time with the Lord.

Talk about sensory overload where all of our senses are being tantalized! Just as we wait in anticipation for the love of our life to call us or to give us endearing compliments. So it is with God. He wants us to spend time with him. God wants our love and time.

Anticipated visits, the expectation of hearing one's voice, and the desire to please the ones we love are the same types of feelings that we should express when communicating with God, who truly is the first real love of our lives. Who else but God has taught us how to love and in turn what to expect? And the good thing about God's love is that it never taps out and we can get refilled, renewed, and replenished at any time. He is always available.

It is important not to allow our pain to distract or hinder us from our praise or destiny. God is worthy of our praise. So when our soul hungers and thirsts for spiritual renewal, even in the midst of going to church, shouting, and praising, it is important to live a purposeful and fulfilled life.

Yes, it is easy to go through the motions without much meaning or movement. However, God has equipped us to live life and to live it more abundantly. "The thief cometh not, but for to steal, and to kill, and to destroy: I am come that they might have **life**, and that they might have it **more abundantly**" (John 10:10, KJV). In order to understand the art of waiting, we must begin to live that meaningful life now.

Write that book you've been putting off, go back

to school, work in your ministry, start up your business, whatever your hands see fit–pursue the work that God has already completed. Identify the **"what"** in your life that you are waiting for and go get it. It is up to you!

"But they that wait upon the Lord shall renew their strength; they shall mount up with wings as eagles; they shall run, and not be weary; and they shall walk, and not faint" (Isaiah 40:31, KJV).

Go forth and be ready for the next move of God. HE is *waiting*!

Spiritual Reflections

Do you remember your first love? How about your first experience loving God? What in your life has kept you from developing a closer relationship with God, your first true love? Are you ready to become reacquainted with God?

RESOURCES FROM HEALTHY LIFE PRESS

Unless otherwise noted on the site itself, shipping is free for all products purchased through *www.healthylifepress.com*.

We've Got Mail: The New Testament Letters in Modern English – As Relevant Today as Ever! by Rev. Warren C. Biebel, Jr. – A modern English paraphrase of the New Testament Letters, sure to inspire in readers a loving appreciation for God's Word. (Printed book: $9.95; PDF eBook: $6.95; both together: $15.00, direct from publisher; eBook reader versions available at *www.Amazon.com*; *www.BN.com*; *www.deepershopping.com*.)

Hearth & Home – Recipes for Life, by Karey Swan (7th Edition) – Far more than a cookbook, this classic is a life book, with recipes for life as well as for great food. Karey describes how to buy and prepare from scratch a wide variety of tantalizing  dishes, while weaving into the book's fabric the wisdom of the ages plus the recipe that she and her husband used to raise their kids. A great gift for Christmas or for a new bride. (Perfect Bound book [8 x 10, glossy cover]: $17.95; PDF eBook: $12.95; both together: $24.95, direct from publisher; eBook reader versions available at *www.Amazon.com*; *www.BN.com*; *www.deepershopping.com*.)

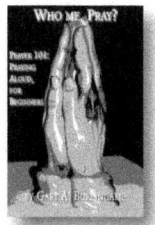
Who Me, Pray? Prayer 101: Praying Aloud, for Beginners, by Gary A. Burlingame – Who Me, Pray? is a practical guide for prayer, based on Jesus' direction in "The Lord's Prayer," with examples provided for use in typical situations where you might be asked or expected to pray in public. (Printed book: $6.95; PDF eBook: $2.99; both together: $7.95, direct from publisher; eBook reader versions available at *www.Amazon-com*; *www.BN.com*; *www.deepershopping.com*.)

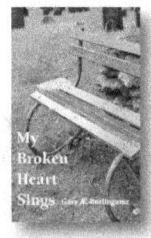
My Broken Heart Sings, the poetry of Gary Burlingame – In 1987, Gary and his wife Debbie lost their son Christopher John, at only six months of age, to a chronic lung disease. This life-changing experience gave them a special heart for helping others through similar loss and pain. (Printed book: $10.95; PDF eBook: $6.95; both together: $13.95; eBook reader versions available at *www.Amazon.com*; *www.BN.com*; *www.deepershopping.com*.)

After Normal: One Teen's Journey Following Her Brother's Death, by Diane Aggen – Based on a journal the author kept following her younger brother's death. It offers helpful insights and understanding for teens facing a similar loss or for those who might wish to understand and help teens facing a similar loss. (Printed book: $11.95; PDF eBook: $6.95; both together: $15.00; eBook reader versions available at *www.Amazon.com*; *www.BN.com*; *www.deepershopping.com*.)

In the Unlikely Event of a Water Landing – Lessons Learned from Landing in the Hudson River, by Andrew Jamison, MD – The author was flying standby on US Airways Flight 1549 toward Charlotte on January 15, 2009, from New York City, where he had been interviewing for a residency position. Little did he know that the next stop would be the Hudson River. Riveting and inspirational, this book would be especially helpful for people in need of hope and encouragement. (Printed book: $8.95; PDF eBook: $6.95; both together: $12.95, direct from publisher; eBook reader versions available at *www.Amazon.com*; *www.BN.com*; *www.deepershopping.com*.)

Finding Martians in the Dark – Everything I Needed to Know About Teaching Took Me Only 30 Years to Learn, by Dan M. Biebel – Packed with wise advice based on hard experience, and laced with humor, this book is a perfect teacher's gift year-round. Susan J. Wegmann, PhD, says, "Biebel's sardonic wit is mellowed by a genuine love for kids and teaching. . . . A Whitman-like sensibility flows through his stories of teaching, learning, and life." (Printed book: $10.95; PDF eBook: $6.95; Together: $15.00; eBook reader versions available at *www.Amazon.com*; *www.BN.com*; *www.deepershopping.com*.)

Because We're Family and **Because We're Friends**, by Gary A. Burlingame – Sometimes things related to faith can be hard to discuss with your family and friends. These booklets are designed to be given as gifts, to help you open the door to discussing spiritual matters with family members and friends who are open to such a conversation. (Printed book: $5.95 each; PDF eBook: $4.95 each; both together: $9.95 [printed & eBook of the same title], direct from publisher; eBook reader versions available at *www.Amazon.com*; *www.BN.com*; *www.deepershopping.com*.)

The Transforming Power of Story: How Telling Your Story Brings Hope to Others and Healing to Yourself, by Elaine Leong Eng, MD, and David B. Biebel, DMin – This book demonstrates, through multiple true life stories, how sharing one's story, especially in a group setting, can bring hope to listeners and healing to the one who shares. Individuals facing difficulties will find this book greatly encouraging. (Printed book: $14.99; PDF eBook: $9.99; both together: $19.99, direct from publisher; eBook reader versions available at *www.Amazon.com*; *www.BN.com*; *www.deepershopping.com*.)

You Deserved a Better Father: Good Parenting Takes a Plan, by Robb Brandt, MD – About parenting by intention, and other lessons the author learned through the loss of his firstborn son. It is especially for parents who believe that bits and pieces of leftover time will be enough for their own children. (Printed book: $10.95 each; PDF eBook: $6.95; both together: $12.95, direct from publisher; eBook reader versions available at *www.Amazon.com*; *www.BN.com*; *www.deepershopping.com*.)

Jonathan, You Left Too Soon, by David B. Biebel, DMin – One pastor's journey through the loss of his son, into the darkness of depression, and back into the light of joy again, emerging with a renewed sense of mission. (Printed book: $12.95; PDF eBook: $5.99; both together: $15.00, direct from publisher; eBook reader versions available at *www.Amazon.com*; *www.BN.com*; *www.deepershopping.com*.)

If God Is So Good, Why Do I Hurt So Bad?, by David B. Biebel, DMin – In this best-selling classic (over 200,000 copies in print worldwide, in five languages) on the subject of loss and renewal, first published in 1989, the author comes alongside people in pain, and shows the way through and beyond it, to joy again. This book has proven helpful to those who are struggling and to those who wish to understand and help. (Printed book: $12.95; PDF eBook: $8.95; both together: $19.95, direct from publisher; eBook reader versions available at *www.Amazon.com*; *www.BN.com*; *www.deepershopping.com*.)

The Spiritual Fitness Checkup for the 50-Something Woman, by Sharon V. King, PhD – Following the stages of a routine medical exam, the author describes ten spiritual fitness "checkups" midlife women can conduct to assess their spiritual health and tone up their relationship with God. Each checkup consists of the author's personal reflections, a Scripture reference for meditation, and a "Spiritual Pulse Check," with exercises readers can use for personal application. (Printed book: $8.95; PDF eBook: $6.95; both together: $12.95, direct from publisher; eBook reader versions available at *www.Amazon.com*; *www.BN.com*; *www.deepershopping.com*.)

The Other Side of Life – Over 60? God Still Has a Plan for You, by Rev. Warren C. Biebel, Jr. – Drawing on biblical examples and his 60-plus years of pastoral experience, Rev. Biebel helps older (and younger) adults understand God's view of aging and the rich life available to everyone who seeks a deeper  relationship with God as they age. Rev. Biebel explains how to: Identify God's ongoing plan for your life; Rely on faith to manage the anxieties of aging; Form positive, supportive relationships; Cultivate patience; Cope with new technologies; Develop spiritual integrity; Understand the effects of dementia; Develop a Christ-centered perspective of aging. (Printed book: $10.95; PDF eBook: $6.95; both together: $15.00, direct from publisher; eBook reader versions available at *www.Amazon.com*; *www.BN.com*; *www.deepershopping.com*.)

 **My Faith, My Poetry**, by Gary A. Burlingame – This unique book of Christian poetry is actually two in one. The first collection of poems, A Day in the Life, explores a working parent's daily journey of faith. The reader is carried from morning to bedtime, from "In the Details," to "I Forgot to Pray," back to "Home Base," and finally to "Eternal Love Divine." The second collection of poems, Come Running, is wonder, joy, and faith wrapped up in words that encourage and inspire the mind and the heart. (Printed book: $10.95; PDF eBook: $6.95; both together: $13.95, direct from publisher; eBook

reader versions available at *www.Amazon.com*; *www.BN.com*; *www.deepershopping.com*.)

On Eagles' Wings, by Sara Eggleston – One woman's life journey from idyllic through chaotic to joy, carried all the way by the One who has promised to never leave us nor forsake us. Remarkable, poignant, moving, and inspiring, this autobiographical account will help many who are facing difficulties that seem too great to overcome or even bear at all. It is proof that Isaiah 40:31 is as true today as when it was penned, "But they that wait upon the LORD shall renew their strength; they shall mount up with wings as eagles; they shall run, and not be weary; and they shall walk, and not faint." (Printed book: $14.95; PDF eBook: $8.95; both together: $22.95, direct from publisher; eBook reader versions available at *www.Amazon.com*; *www.BN.com*; *www.deepershopping.com*.)

Richer Descriptions, by Gary A. Burlingame – A unique and handy manual, covering all nine human senses in seven chapters, for Christian speakers and writers. Exercises and a speaker's checklist equip speakers to engage their audiences in a richer experience. Writing examples and a writer's guide help writers bring more life to the characters and scenes of their stories. Bible references encourage a deeper appreciation of being created by God for a sensory existence. (Printed book: $15.95; PDF eBook: $8.95; both together: $22.95, direct from publisher; eBook reader versions available at *www.Amazon.com*; *www.BN.com*; *www.deepershopping.com*.)

Treasuring Grace, by Rob Plumley and Tracy Roberts – This novel was inspired by a dream. Liz Swanson's life isn't quite what she'd imagined, but she considers herself lucky. She has a good husband, beautiful children, and fulfillment outside of her home through volunteer work. On some days she doesn't even notice the dull ache in her heart. While she's preparing for their summer kickoff at Lake George, the ache disappears and her sudden happiness is mistaken for anticipation of their weekend. However, as the family heads north, there are clouds on the horizon that have nothing to do with the weather. Only Liz's daughter, who's found some of her mother's hidden journals, has any idea what's wrong. But by the end of the weekend, there will be no escaping the truth or its painful buried secrets. (Printed: $12.95; PDF eBook: $7.95; both together: $19.95, direct from publisher; eBook reader versions available at *www.Amazon.com*; *www.BN.com*; *www.deepershopping.com*.)

Life's A Symphony, by Mary Z. Smith – When Kate Spence Cooper receives the news that her husband, Jack, has been killed in the war, she and her young son Jeremy move back to Crawford Wood, Tennessee to be closer to family. Since Jack's death Kate feels that she's lost trust in everyone, including God. Will she  ever find her way back to the only One whom she can always depend upon? And what about Kate's match making brother, Chance? The cheeky man has other ideas on how to bring happiness into his sister's life once more. (Printed book: $12.95; PDF eBook: $7.95; both together: $19.95, direct from publisher; eBook reader versions available at *www.Amazon.com*; *www.BN.com*; *www.deepershopping.com*.)

From Orphan to Physician – The Winding Path, by Chun-Wai Chan, MD – From the foreword: "In this book, Dr. Chan describes how his family escaped to Hong Kong, how they survived in utter poverty, and how he went from being an orphan to graduating from Harvard Medical School and becoming a cardiologist. The writing is fluent, easy to read and understand. The sequence of events is realistic, emotionally moving, spiritually touching, heart-warming, and thought provoking. The book illustrates . . . how one must have faith in order to walk through life's winding path." (Printed book: $14.95; PDF eBook: $8.95; both together: $22.95, direct from publisher; eBook reader versions available at *www.Amazon.com*; *www.BN.com*; *www.deepershopping.com*.)

12 Parables, by Wayne Faust – Timeless Christian stories about doubt, fear, change, grief, and more. Using tight, entertaining prose, professional musician and comedy performer Wayne Faust manages to deal with difficult concepts in a simple, straightforward way. These are stories you can read aloud over and over—to your spouse, your family, or in a group setting. Packed with emotion and just enough mystery to keep you wondering, while providing lots of points to ponder and discuss when you're through, these stories relate the gospel in the tradition of the greatest speaker of parables the world has ever known, who appears in them often. (Printed book: $14.95; PDF eBook: $8.95; both together: $22.95, direct from publisher; eBook reader versions available at *www.Amazon.com*; *www.BN.com*; *www.deepershopping.com*.)

**The Answer is Always "Jesus,"** by Aram Haroutunian, who gave children's sermons for 15 years at a large church in Golden, Colorado—well over 500 in all. This book contains 74 of his most unforgettable presentations—due to the children's responses. Pastors, homeschoolers, parents who often lead family devotions, or other storytellers will find these stories, along with comments about props and how to prepare and present them, an invaluable asset in reconnecting with the simplest, most profound truths of Scripture, and then to envision how best to communicate these so even a child can understand them. (Printed book: $12.95; PDF eBook: $8.95; both together: $19.95, direct from publisher; eBook reader versions available at *www.Amazon.com*; *www.BN.com*; *www.deepershopping.com*.)

Handbook of Faith, by Rev. Warren C. Biebel, Jr. – The New York Times World 2011 Almanac claimed that there are 2 billion, 200 thousand Christians in the world, with "Christians" being defined as "followers of Christ." The original 12 followers of Christ changed the world; indeed, they changed the history of the 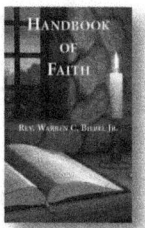 world. So this author, a pastor with over 60 years' experience, poses and answers this logical question: "If there are so many 'Christians' on this planet, why are they so relatively ineffective in serving the One they claim to follow?" Answer: Because, unlike Him, they do not know and trust the Scriptures, implicitly. This little volume will help you do that. (Printed book: $8.95; PDF eBook: $6.95; both together: $13.95, direct from publisher; eBook reader versions available at *www.Amazon.com*; *www.BN.com*; *www.deepershopping.com*.)

Pieces of My Heart, by David L. Wood – Eighty-two lessons from normal everyday life. David's hope is that these stories will spark thoughts about God's constant involvement and intervention in our lives and stir a sense of how much He cares about every detail that is important to us. The piece missing represents his son, Daniel, who died in a fire shortly before his first birthday. (Printed book: $16.95; PDF eBook: $8.95; both together: $24.95, direct from publisher; eBook reader versions available at *www.Amazon.com*; *www.BN.com*; *www.deepershopping.com*.)

Dream House, by Justa Carpenter – Written by a New England builder of several hundred homes, the idea for this book came to him one day as he was driving that came to him one day as was driving from one job site to another. He pulled over and recorded it so he would remember it, and now you will re-  member it, too, if you believe, as he does, that ". . . He who has begun a good work in you will complete it until the day of Jesus Christ." (Printed book: $10.95; PDF eBook: $6.95; both together: $13.95, direct from publisher; eBook reader versions available at *www.Amazon.com*; *www.BN.com*; *www.deepershopping.com*.)

A Simply Homemade Clean, by homesteader Lisa Barthuly – "Somewhere along the path, it seems we've lost our gumption, the desire to make things ourselves," says the author. "Gone are the days of 'do it yourself.' Really . . . why bother? There are a slew of retailers just waiting for us with anything and everything we could need; packaged up all pretty, with no thought or effort required. It is the manifestation of 'progress' . . . right?" I don't buy that!" Instead, Lisa describes how to make safe and effective cleansers for home, laundry, and body right in your own home. This saves money and avoids exposure to harmful chemicals often found in commercially produced cleansers. (Printed book: $12.99; PDF eBook: $6.95; both together: $14.95, direct from publisher; **full-color printed book: $16.99, at *www.healthylifepress.com***; eBook reader versions available at *www.Amazon.com*; *www.BN.com*; *www.deepershopping.com*.)

The Secret of Singing Springs, by Monte Swan – One Colorado family's treasure-hunting adventure along the trail of Jesse James. The Secret of Singing Springs is written to capture for children and their parents the spirit of the hunt—the hunt for treasure as in God's Truth, which is the objective of walking the Way of Wisdom that is described in Proverbs. (Printed book: $12.95, PDF eBook: $9.99; both together: $19.99, direct from publisher; eBook reader versions available at *www.Amazon.com*; *www.BN.com*; *www.deepershopping.com*.)

God Loves You Circle, by Michelle Johnson – Daily inspiration for your deeper walk with Christ. This collection of short stories of Christian living will make you laugh, make you cry, but most of all make you contemplate—the meaning and value of walking with the Master moment-by-moment, day-by-day. (Printed book: $12.95; full-color PDF eBook: $9.99; both together: $19.99, direct from publisher; eBook reader versions available at *www.Amazon.com*; *www.BN.com*; *www.deepershopping.com*; **Full-color printed book: $17.95, direct from publisher.**)

Our God-Given Senses, by Gary A. Burlingame – Did you know humans have NINE senses? The Bible draws on these senses to reveal spiritual truth. We are to taste and see that the Lord is a good. We are to carry the fragrance of Christ. Our faith is produced upon hearing. Jesus asked Thomas to touch him. God created us for a sensory experience and that is what you will find in this book. (Printed book: $12.99; PDF eBook: $9.99; both together: $19.99, direct from publisher; eBook reader versions available at *www.Amazon.com*; *www.BN.com*; *www.deepershopping.com*.)

I AM – Transformed in Him (Volume 1) – by Diana Burg and Kim Tapfer, a meditative women's Bible study on the I AM statements of Christ in two 6-week volumes or one 12-week volume (12-week volume available 2014). Throughout this six week study you will begin to unearth the treasure trove of riches that are found within God's name, I AM WHO I AM. (Printed book: $12.99; PDF eBook: $9.99; both together: $19.99, direct from publisher; **AUTOGRAPHED COPIES OF VOLUME 1 ARE AVAILABLE FROM THE PUBLISHER: *www.healthylifepress.com*.** eBook reader versions available at *www.Amazon.com*; *www.BN.com*; *www.deepershopping.com*.)

VOWS, a Romantic novel by F. F. Whitestone – When the police cruiser pulled up to the curb outside, Faith Framingham's heart skipped a beat, for she could see that Chuck, who should have been driving, was not in the vehicle. Chuck's partner, Sandy, stepped out slowly. Sandy's pursed lips and ashen face spoke volumes. Faith waited by the front door, her hands clasped tightly, to counter the fact that her mind was already reeling. "Love never fails." A compelling story. (Printed book: $12.99; PDF eBook: $9.99; both together, $19.99, direct from publisher; eBook reader versions available at *www.Amazon.com*; *www.BN.com*; *www.deepershopping.com*.)

Worth the Cost?, by Jack Tsai, MD – The author was happily on his way to obtaining the American Dream until he decided to take seriously Jesus' command to "Come, follow me." Join him as he explores the cost of medical education and Christian discipleship. Planning to serve God in your future vocation?  Take care that your desires do not get side-tracked by the false promises of this world. What you should be doing now so when you are done with your training you will still want to serve God. (Printed book: $12.99, PDF eBook: $9.99; both together: $19.99, direct from publisher; eBook reader versions available at *www.Amazon.com*; *www.BN.com*; *www.deepershopping.com*.)

Unless otherwise noted on the site itself, shipping is free for all products purchased through
www.healthylifepress.com.

Nature: God's Second Book – An Essential Link to Restoring Your Personal Health and Wellness: Body, Mind, and Spirit, by Elvy P. Rolle – An inspirational book that looks at nature across the seasons of nature and of life. It uses the biblical Emmaus Journey as an analogy for life's journey, and offers ideas for using nature appreciation and exploration to reduce life's stresses. The author shares her personal story of how she came to grips with this concept after three trips to the emergency room. (**Full-color printed book: $12.99, direct from publisher**; PDF eBook $8.99; both together: $16.99, direct from publisher only; eBook reader versions available at *www.Amazon.com*; *www.BN.com*; *www.deepershopping.com*.)

He Waited, by LaDonna Cooper – Inspires readers to wait upon the Lord for His best for them; stresses the importance of putting God's purpose above one's own; emphasizes that God's love is unconditional; demonstrates the wisdom of waiting, through a combination of positive insights, encouragement,

biblical examples and principles. Decorated with original poetry by the author. For singles and others who are waiting. Distributed primarily through *www.Amazon.com*. (Printed book: $10.99; PDF eBook: $9.99; both together: $15.99, direct from publisher; eBook reader versions available at *www.Amazon.com*; *www.BN.com*; *www.deepershopping.com*.)

Seasonal

The Big Black Book – What the Christmas Tree Saw, by Rev. Warren C. Biebel, Jr. – An original Christmas story, from the perspective of the Christmas tree. This little book is especially suitable for parents to read to their children at Christmas time or all year-round. (Full-color printed book: $9.95; PDF eBook: $4.95; both together: $10.95, direct from publisher; eBook reader versions available at *www.Amazon.com*; *www.BN.com*; *www.deepershopping.com*.)

About Healthy Life Press

Healthy Life Press was founded with a primary goal of helping previously unpublished authors to get their works to market, and to reissue worthy, previously published works that were no longer available. Our mission is to help people toward optimal vitality by providing resources promoting physical, emotional, spiritual, and relational health as viewed from a Christian perspective. We see health as a verb, and achieving optimal health as a process—a crucial process for followers of Christ if we are to love the Lord with all our heart, soul, mind, AND strength, and our neighbors as ourselves—for as long as He leaves us here. We are a collaborative and cooperative small Christian publisher.

For information about publishing with us, e-mail: *healthylifepress@aol.com*.

Recommended Resources – Books

52 Ways to Feel Great Today, by David B. Biebel, DMin, James E. Dill, MD, and Bobbie Dill, RN – **Increase Your Vitality, Improve your Outlook.** Simple, fun, inexpensive things you can do to increase your vitality and improve your outlook. Why live an "ordinary" life when you could be experiencing the extraordinary? Don't settle for good enough when "great" is such a short stretch further. Make today great! (Printed book: List: $14.99, Sale: $5.99.)

New Light on Depression, a CBA Gold Medallion winner, by David B. Biebel, DMin, and Harold Koenig, MD – The most comprehensive Christian resource on a subject that is more common than we might wish. Hope for those with depression and help for those who love them. (Printed book: $14.99.)

Your Mind at Its Best – 40 Ways To Keep Your Brain Sharp, by David B. Biebel, DMin; James E. Dill, MD; and, Bobbie Dill, RN – Everyone wants their mind to function at high levels throughout life. In 40 easy-to-understand chapters, readers will discover a wide variety of tips and tricks to keep their minds sharp. Synthesizing science and self-help, Your Mind at Its Best makes fascinating neurological discoveries understandable and immediately applicable to readers of any age. (Printed book: List: $13.99, Sale $5.99.)

Recommended Resources – Pro-Life DVD Series

See *www.healthylifepress.com* (select "DVD")

Eyewitness 2 (Public School Version) – This DVD has been used in many public schools. It is a fascinating journey through 38 weeks of pregnancy, showing developing babies via cutting edge digital ultrasound technology. Separate chapters allow viewing distinct segments individually. (List Price: $34.95; Sale Price: $24.95.)

Window To the Womb (Pregnancy Care & Counseling Version) – Facts about fetal development, abortion complications, post-abortion syndrome, and healing. Separate chapters allow selection of specialized presentations to accommodate the needs and time constraints of their situations. (List Price: $34.95; Sale Price: $24.95.)

COMBINATION Offer: Eyewitness 2 and Window to the Womb 2 (List Price: $84.90; Sale Price: $49.95.)

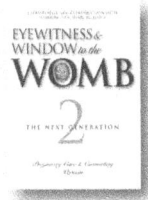

Window To The Womb (2 DVD Disc Set) Disc 1: Ian Donald (1910-1987) "A Prophetic Legacy;" Disc 2: "A Journey from Death To Life" (50 min) – Includes history of sonography and its increasing impact against abortion—more than 80% of expectant parents who "see" their developing baby choose for life. Perfect for counseling and education in Pregnancy Centers, Christian schools, homeschools, and churches. (List: $49.95; Sale: $34.95.)

www.ingramcontent.com/pod-product-compliance
Lightning Source LLC
Chambersburg PA
CBHW052104070526
44584CB00017B/2322